TABLE OF CONTENTS

INTRODUCTION

Who doesn't love the smell and aroma of fresh home made bread? Who doesn't like to enjoy its texture, taste and richness? If you are one of us, then this next recipes collection is exactly what you need. You are about to discover some of the best and most delicious bread recipes. All these tasty breads are right here, gathered in just one and simple journal available for everyone.

We gathered here some bread recipes that anyone can make in the comfort of their own home. All these breads contain simple and easy to obtain ingredients and the recipes are all easy to follow. So, even if you are not an expert in the kitchen, you will still be able to make these delicious breads.

Everyone will love these breads and you will really impress your loved ones and friends with these wonderful recipes.

If you are convinced that you want to learn how to bake delicious breads, then all you need to do is to check out this great journal. Don't wait any longer. Get your hands on this simple and easy collection and start baking right away. It will be a fun and entertaining activity for the whole family.

What are you still waiting for? Get started right away and enjoy some rich and delightful bread as soon as possible. Enjoy this culinary trip and have fun with this experience! It will be an un-forgetful one for sure!

USEFUL TIPS

Before getting started and actually baking the bread, there are some simple but important things you should know about it. This includes some basic principles to use in baking bread, what flour to use, how much water, making the sourdough and other similar things.

That is why we gathered this information for you. So, *here is what you need to know.*

The first thing you do when you begin making a bread is the sourdough starter. This requires some time and a little effort from your part but it is totally worth it. This is not a complex action and even an amateur can do it! It's actually easier than you can imagine.

When you receive the sourdough culture, you just have to activate and feed the starter with flour. You can use different types of flour and even combinations of 2 types of flour together. You can use white flour, wheat, rye one, etc.

When you start making the sourdough starter always use the least amount of flour required and add more as you obtain your dough. Try to add the flour gradually and not all at once. It will help you obtain the best dough.

Here are some useful tips for your sourdough culture:

- you must take care of your starter by refreshing it on a regular basis
- if you don't use the starter you can keep it in a fridge and it will be as good as new when you use it again;
- you can make the sourdough starter smell nice by using citrus or fruity flavors;
- you must give the sourdough starter some oxygen and therefore you have to stir it constantly;
- use the best water for your sourdough starter: if your tap water contains too much chlorine, you should use bottled one instead;
- if your sourdough starter changes its color and if it becomes too fluffy you should get rid of it and start all over again;
- never neglect your starter. It's literally like a baby. It needs constant care and maintenance if you want to get the best bread.

One last thing you should know about the sourdough starter is how to test it. The best test is the float test for both sourdough starter and yeast dough. When the yeast starts to work it produces carbon dioxide. This is what it make the dough rise and become light and fluffy.

The float test is this: if the dough just begun to rise it will sink when dropped in water. The longer the dough rises, the lighter it becomes and it will float when dropped in water. That's a trick not everyone knows or uses but it can be a useful one for amateurs that are baking for the first time.

Now, it's time for you to knead the dough. This should be a simple action that anyone can make. It just involves working the dough until it's elastic enough. You need an elastic dough in order to make the bread rise.

When you knead, you should work on a lightly floured working surface. Knead the dough for 10-20 minutes until you get the elastic dough you need.

The next thing your dough needs is enough time aside in order to rise and to allow the sourdough culture to react. The only thing you have to do is to gather the kneaded dough, shape it, cover it with a cloth and keep it in a warm place to rise.

Baking is the last step and the easiest one. Just bake your bread until its internal temperature reaches 210 degrees F. Always remember this: The bread should be cold enough before cutting and serving it.

As you can see, there are some tips and tricks you can use when baking the bread. We gathered here some simple ones you can use right away. We guarantee that if you use our tips you will enjoy the best bread one can make at home.

SOURDOUGH STORAGE

This is also an important aspect for you to know and keep in mind when working with sourdough starter.

So, let's find out together how to store a sourdough starter. If you feed your starter daily, once or twice a day it will function in a very effective way.

You can keep your sourdough starter in a plastic container, in a glass jar, in a pint jar and even in a covered pot. Our recommendation is to keep the starter in the fridge but this is not a requirement. You can also keep it in a cold dark place in the kitchen and open it only when you need to feed it.

If you decide to not use your starter for now, you can store it by drying it. Just spread it on 2 pieces of parchment paper as thinly as you can using a spatula, leave it at room temperature to completely dry (it will take a day or two), then peel it piece by piece off the parchment and keep it I a plastic bag until you need it again.

As you can see, it's pretty easy to store your sourdough for a longer time. Just use our tips and you will use your sourdough in the most effective and easy way.

Now that you know how to get started with the sourdough, how to store it and which tips and tricks can make this culinary experience easier, it's time to get to work and start baking.

RUSTIC LOAVES

RUSTIC SOURDOUGH BREAD

Prep time: 2 h and 40 min | Cooking time: 30 min | Servings: 2 loaves

INGREDIENTS:
1 cup sourdough starter	5 cups white flour
1 and ½ cups water (warm)	2 tsp instant yeast
2 tsp salt	

DIRECTIONS:
In a large bowl, mix the sourdough starter with the water and the other ingredients, stir well until you obtain a dough, cover the bowl and allow the dough to rise for 1 h and 30 min. Divide the dough in half, shape 2 loaves, place them on a parchment-lined baking sheet, cover and leave the dough to rise for another h. Cook in preheated oven at 425 degrees F for 30 min, cool down.

NUTRITION:
calories 80, fat 0, fiber 1, carbs 17, protein 5

RUSTIC HONEY BREAD

Prep time: 5 h and 10 min | Cooking time: 40 min | Servings: 1 loaf

INGREDIENTS:
3 cups all purpose flour	1 and ¼ cups warm water
¾ cup active sourdough starter	1 tbsp honey
	1 and ½ tsp salt

DIRECTIONS:
In a large bowl, mix the flour with the other ingredients, stir well until you obtain a dough, cover the bowl and allow the dough to rise for 5 h. Transfer to a loaf pan and bake at 450 degrees F for 40 min. Leave the loaf to cool down, slice and serve.

NUTRITION:
calories 119, fat 0.2, fiber 0.8, carbs 24, protein 3.2

CRUSTY BREAD

Prep time: 2 h and 10 min | Cooking time: 25 min | Servings: 2 loaves

INGREDIENTS:
1 and ½ tbsp instant yeast	1 tbsp salt
6 and ½ cups all purpose flour	3 cups warm milk
	1 tsp turmeric powder

DIRECTIONS:
In a bowl mix the flour with the yeast and the other ingredients, stir until you obtain a dough, cover the bowl and allow to rise for 2 h in a warm place. Shape 2 loaves, arrange them on a baking sheet lined with parchment paper and bake at 430 degrees F for 25 min.

NUTRITION:
calories 100, fat 4.3, fiber 0.6, carbs 4, protein 3.4

MEXICAN RUSTIC LOAF

Prep time: 2 h and 10 min | Cooking time: 20 min | Servings: 2 loaves

INGREDIENTS:
4 cups white flour	1 tsp cinnamon powder
2/3 cup sugar	1 egg
1 cup milk	1 tsp vanilla extract
½ cup butter	
2 tsp dry yeast	

DIRECTIONS:
In a large bowl, mix the flour with the sugar, milk and the

other ingredients, stir until you obtain a dough, cover and leave aside for 2 h. Shape the loaves, place them on a baking sheet lined with parchment paper and bake at 435 degrees F for 20 min. Cool down, slice and serve.

NUTRITION:
calories 121, fat 1.2, fiber 2.3, carbs 0.3, protein 1.1

AMERICAN LOAF

Prep time: 1 h and 30 min | Cooking time: 1 h | Servings: 1 loaf

INGREDIENTS:

3 and ½ cups white flour	3 tbsp honey
2 tsp salt	2 tbsp butter, melted
1/3 cup water	2 tsp dry yeast
1 cup warm milk	1 tbsp vegetable oil

DIRECTIONS:
In a bowl, mix the flour with the salt, water, milk and the other ingredients, stir until you obtain a dough, knead for 10 min, cover the bowl and leave aside to rise for 1 h. Shape the loaf, arrange it on a baking sheet lined with parchment paper and leave aside to rise for 20 min more. Bake at 350 degrees F for 1 h, cool down, slice and serve.

NUTRITION:
calories 100, fat 1.2, fiber 1, carbs 3.3, protein 3

ETHIOPIAN BREAD

Prep time: 10 min | Cooking time: 10 min | Servings: 6

INGREDIENTS:

2 cups white flour	2 cups sparkling water
Juice of 2 limes	1 tbsp baking powder
1 tsp salt	

Cooking spray

DIRECTIONS:
In a bowl, mix the flour with salt, water, baking powder and lime juice and stir well. Grease a pan with cooking spray, heat up over medium heat, pour ½ cups of the bread batter you've made, spread and cook for 2 min on each side. Repeat with the remaining batter, cool the breads down, roll and serve them.
Nutrition/ roll: calories 89, fat 0.5, fiber 0, carbs 1, protein 1.1

SPICED RUSTIC BREAD

Prep time: 1 h and 10 min | Cooking time: 1 h | Servings: 1 loaf

INGREDIENTS:

1 egg, whisked	ground
½ cup honey	1 tsp cloves, ground
¼ cup warm water	1 tsp cinnamon powder
4 cups white flour	2 tsp salt
1 tsp coriander, ground	3 tbsp butter, melted
1 tsp ginger,	

DIRECTIONS:
I a bowl, mix the flour with coriander and the other dry ingredients and stir. In a separate large bowl, mix the egg with the wet ingredients and stir again. Combine the 2 mixtures and start kneading until you obtain an elastic dough, cover the bowl and leave aside for 1 h. Shape your loaf, arrange on a baking sheet lined with parchment paper and bake at 300 degrees F for 1 h. Cool down, slice and serve.

NUTRITION:
calories 80, fat 2, fiber 0.7, carbs 1.1, protein 0.8

INDIAN BREADS

Prep time: 1 h and 30 min | Cooking time: 10 min | Servings: 12

INGREDIENTS:
4 tbsp sugar
2 tsp salt
4 cups white flour
1 tsp dry yeast
1 cup warm milk
1 egg, whisked
4 tbsp butter, melted

DIRECTIONS:
In a large bowl, mix the sugar with salt, flour and yeast and stir. Add the rest of the ingredients, knead the mix until you obtain an elastic dough, cover the bowl and allow it to rise for 1 h. Divide the dough into 12 balls and allow them to rise for 30 min more. Heat up your grill over medium-high heat, flatten the balls, cook them for 4 min one each side and serve.

NUTRITION:
calories 76, fat 1.2, fiber 0.8, carbs 1, protein 1.2

RUSTIC GERMAN BREAD

Prep time: 5 h | Cooking time: 45 min | Servings: 1 big loaf

INGREDIENTS:
1 cup all purpose flour
1 and ½ cups water
1 tsp instant
yeast
3 tbsp honey
2 tbsp caraway seeds
1 tbsp olive oil

DIRECTIONS:
In a bowl, mix the flour with the water, instant yeast and the other ingredients, knead well, cover and leave aside for 2 h. Transfer the dough to a floured working surface, knead for 10 more min and leave covered to rise for 2 more h. Shape a big round bread, arrange on a baking sheet lined with parchment paper, cover

and leave aside to rise for 1 more h. Bake at 400 degrees F for 45 min, cool down, slice and serve.

NUTRITION:
calories 99, fat 1.2 fiber 2.1, carbs 1.4, protein 2

PITA BREAD

Prep time: 3 h | Cooking time: 10 min | Servings: 8

INGREDIENTS:
2 cups white flour
1 cup warm water
1 tsp salt
½ tsp black pepper
1 tsp dry yeast
2 and ½ tbsp olive oil

DIRECTIONS:
In a bowl, mix the flour with water, salt, pepper, yeast and ½ tbsp oil, knead until you obtain an elastic dough, cover the bowl and leave aside to rise for 2 h. Divide the dough in 8 balls, cover the bowl again and leave aside to rise for 1 more h. Heat up a pan with the remaining oil over medium-high heat, flatten a ball into a circle, place in the pan and cook for 5 min on each side. Repeat with the rest of the dough.

NUTRITION:
calories 45, fat 0.1, fiber 1, carbs 0.7, protein 0.6

IRISH LOAF

Prep time: 1 h and 10 min | Cooking time: 50 min | Serving: 1 loaf

INGREDIENTS:
4 tbsp sugar
½ cup margarine
1 cup buttermilk
4 cups white
flour
1 tsp salt
1 tsp baking soda
1 egg, whisked

DIRECTIONS:
In a large bowl mix the sugar with the flour, salt and baking soda, stir and leave aside for 10 min. Add the rest of the ingredients, stir until you obtain a dough, cover the bowl and leave aside to rise for 1 h. Transfer to a loaf pan, introduce in the oven and bake at 375 degrees F for 50 min. Cool the loaf dough, slice and serve.

NUTRITION:
calories 99, fat 1.1, fiber 0.8, carbs 1.9, protein 0.6

ISRAELI LOAF

Prep time: 3 h and 30 min | Cooking time: 40 min | Servings: 3 loaves

INGREDIENTS:

8 cups white flour	1 tbsp dry yeast
1 tsp poppy seeds	4 tbsp vegetable oil
2 and ½ cups warm water	3 eggs, whisked

DIRECTIONS:
In a large bowl, mix the flour with yeast and poppy seeds and stir. Add the rest of the ingredients, stir well, knead the dough for 15 min, cover the bowls and leave aside to rise for 3 h. Divide the dough into 3 loaf pans and leave them aside to rise for 15 more min. Bake at 400 degrees F for 40 min, cool down and serve.

NUTRITION:
calories 101, fat 1.2, fiber 0, carbs 1.6, protein 1.1

RUSSIAN BREAD

Prep time: 3 h and 10 min | Cooking time: 40 min | Servings: 2 loaves

INGREDIENTS:

3 cups white flour	1 tbsp coffee
2 cups warm water	1 tsp salt
2 tbsp cider vinegar	1 tsp fennel seeds, crushed
½ tsp coriander, ground	2 tbsp corn syrup
1 tbsp brown sugar	2 tsp dry yeast
	3 tbsp butter, melted

DIRECTIONS:
In a large bowl, mix the flour with coriander, sugar, coffee, salt, fennel and yeast and stir well. In a separate bowl, mix the water with the rest of the ingredients, stir as well and leave aside for 10 min. Combine the 2 mixtures, stir until you obtain a dough, knead, cover and leave aside for 2 h. Shape the 2 loaves, divide them in loaf pans and leave aside to rise for 1 more h. Bake at 400 degrees for 40 min and serve completely cold.

NUTRITION:
calories 110, fat 1.4, fiber 1, carbs 2, protein 2.2

FRENCH LOAF

Prep time: 2 h and 10 min | Cooking time: 45 min | Servings: 2 loaves

INGREDIENTS:

1 tbsp yeast	1 tsp cumin, ground
2 cups warm water	1 tsp ginger, ground
1 tbsp vegetable oil	5 cups white flour
1 tsp nutmeg, ground	1 tbsp sugar

DIRECTIONS:
In a bowl mix the flour with the cumin, nutmeg, ginger, sugar and the yeast and stir well. Add the rest of the ingredients, stir

and knead the dough, cover and leave aside in a warm place for 2 h. Transfer the dough to 2 loaf pans, and bake at 400 degrees F for 45 min. Cool the loaf down, slice and serve.

NUTRITION:
calories 99, fat 1.2, fiber 1, carbs 2.1, protein 0.9

CRISPY HUNGARIAN BREAD

Prep time: 3 h and 30 min | Cooking time: 50 min | Servings: 1 loaf

INGREDIENTS:
2 tsp dry yeast
4 cups white flour
1 tsp salt
1 and ½ cup warm almond milk
1 egg yolk
1 tbsp cumin, ground
1 tbsp sugar
1 tbsp vegetable oil

DIRECTIONS:
In a bowl, mix the flour with salt, cumin, sugar and yeast and stir well. Add the rest of the ingredients, knead for 15 min, cover the bowl and leave aside for 3 h. Transfer to a loaf pan, leave the pan aside for 30 min more and bake at 390 degrees F for 50 min. Cool the loaf down, slice and serve.

NUTRITION:
calories 110, fat 1.2, fiber 2, carbs 1.2, protein 2.1

HERBED LOAF

Prep time: 2 h and 10 min | Cooking time: 1 h | Servings: 1 loaf

INGREDIENTS:
2 tsp dry yeast
1 cup warm milk
2 tbsp butter,
melted
3 tbsp honey
3 cups white flour

1 tsp salt
2/3 cup chives, chopped
½ tsp black pepper

DIRECTIONS:
In a bowl, mix the flour with the yeast, salt, pepper and chives and stir. Add the rest of the ingredients, knead the dough for 15 min, cover the bowls and leave aside to rise for 2 h. Transfer to a loaf pan, bake at 380 degrees F for 1 h, cool down, slice and serve.

NUTRITION:
calories 88, fat 0.2, fiber 1.1, carbs 1.2, protein 1

SIMPLE BAGUETTE

Prep time: 2 h | Cooking time: 40 min | Servings: 3 baguettes

INGREDIENTS:
1 cup white flour
¼ cup physsilium husk
2 tbsp baking soda
¼ cup corn starch
1 tsp salt
1 egg, whisked
1 tsp turmeric powder
1 and ½ cups warm water
1 tsp dry yeast
1 tbsp baking fibers

DIRECTIONS:
In a bowl, mix the flour with the baking soda, corn starch and the other ingredients except the egg and the water and stir. Add the egg and stir the mix again. Add the water gradually and stir until you obtain a dough. Cover the bowl with the dough and leave aside in a warm place for 2 h. Shape 3 logs out of this dough, arrange them on a lined baking sheet, leave them 10 more min to rise and then bake them at 400 degrees F for 40 min. Cool the baguettes down and serve.

SPICY RUSTIC BREAD

Prep time: 2 h and 10 min | Cooking time: 50 min | Servings: 2 loaves

INGREDIENTS:
¼ cup sriracha sauce
½ cup warm water
1 egg, whisked
3 cups white flour
1 tbsp vegetable oil
1 tsp salt
1 tsp butter, melted

DIRECTIONS:
In a bowl, mix the flour with the salt and the other ingredients and stir well until you obtain a dough. Transfer the dough to a working surface, and knead for 10 min. Return the dough to a bowl, cover and rise for 2 h. Divide the dough into 2 loaf pans and bake at 390 degrees F for 50 min. Cool the breads down, slice and serve.

RUSTIC CHEESE BREAD

Prep time: 1 h and 30 min | Cooking time: 40 min | Servings: 2 loaves

INGREDIENTS:
2 tsp baking powder
2 cups white flour
1 tsp salt
¼ cup sugar
1 cup almond milk
3 tbsp vegetable oil
1 cup cheddar cheese, grated

DIRECTIONS:
In a bowl, mix the flour with the salt, baking powder and the other ingredients, stir, knead the dough, cover the bowl and allow it to rise for 1 h. Divide the dough into 2 loaf pans and allow them to rise for 30 min more. Bake the bread at 420 degrees F for 40 min.

POTATO BREAD

Prep time: 2 h and 10 min | Cooking time: 50 min | Servings: 2 loaves

INGREDIENTS:
1 and ½ cups warm water
2 tbsp shortening
2 tbsp sugar
2 tsp dry yeast
1 potato, baked, peeled and grated
4 cups white flour
1 tsp salt

DIRECTIONS:
In a bowl, mix the water with the shortening, sugar and the other ingredients, stir, knead well, cover the bowl and leave aside to rise for 2 h. Divide the dough into 2 loaves, leave them to rise for 10 more min and bake at 395 degrees F for 50 min. Cool down, slice and serve.

WHOLE GRAIN BREADS RECIPES

FLAX BREAD

Prep time: 10 min | Cooking time: 45 min | Servings: 1 bread

INGREDIENTS:

1 cup flaxseed meal	1 tsp baking soda
4 eggs, whisked	1 tsp salt
1 cup coconut flour	1 tbsp apple cider vinegar
1 tsp baking powder	½ cup warm water

DIRECTIONS:

In a bowl, mix the coconut flour with flaxseed meal and the other ingredients except the eggs and the water and stir. Add the water and eggs, stir and knead until you obtain a dough. Transfer it to a loaf pan and bake at 350 degrees F for 40 min before cooling and serving.

NUTRITION:

calories 300, fat 12, fiber 1.2, carbs 4.3, protein 9.2

FLAX STEVIA BREAD

Prep time: 10 min | Cooking time: 20 min | Servings: 1 loaf

INGREDIENTS:

1 tbsp baking powder	whisked
1 and ½ cup protein isolate	1 whole egg, whisked
½ tsp salt	1 cup water
2 cups flax seed meal	¼ cup stevia
4 egg whites,	2 tbsp coconut oil, melted

DIRECTIONS:

In a bowl, mix the flax seed meal with the protein isolate and the other dry ingredients and stir. Add the remaining wet ingredi-

ents, stir and knead the obtained dough. Transfer to a big loaf pan and bake at 370 degrees F for 20 min. Cool down, slice and serve.

NUTRITION:

calories 87, fat 1.2, fiber 0.7, carbs 3, protein 2.2

WHEAT AND ALMOND FOCACCIA

Prep time: 2 h | Cooking time: 40 min | Servings: 2 focaccia

INGREDIENTS:

1 cup wheat flour	minced
1 cup almond flour	1 tbsp baking powder
½ tsp salt	5 eggs, whisked
½ tsp cayenne pepper	1 tbsp rosemary, dried
½ cup olive oil	Cooking spray
2 garlic cloves,	

DIRECTIONS:

In a bowl, mix the wheat flour with the almond flour and the other ingredients except the oil and stir well. Add the oil gradually and stir everything well again. Pour this into 2 square pans greased with the cooking spray, bake at 330 degrees F for 40 min, cool down and serve.

NUTRITION:

calories 243, fat 5.4, fiber 4.4, carbs 5.4, protein 3.2

CORN SHORTBREAD

Prep time: 30 min | Cooking time: 15 min | Servings: 8

INGREDIENTS:

2 cups corn flour	4 tbsp sugar
5 tbsp ghee, melt	1 tbsp lemon juice
1 tbsp lemon zest, grated	1 tsp vanilla extract
	1 tsp baking

powder   dried
1 tsp rosemary,

DIRECTIONS:
In a bowl, mix the flour with
the lemon zest, sugar, baking
powder and rosemary and stir.
Add gradually the other ingredients, stir well until you obtain a
dough, make a log, wrap in plastic and keep in the freezer for
30 min. Cut the log into circles,
arrange on a baking sheet lined
with parchment paper and cook
at 370 degrees F for 15 min before cooling down and serving.

NUTRITION/ PIECE:
calories 100, fat 2.3, fiber 2.3,
carbs 3.4, protein 4.3

RYE PUMPKIN BREAD

Prep time: 10 min | Cooking
time: 1 h and 20 min | Servings:
2 loaves

INGREDIENTS:
1 and ½ cups   milk, warm
rye flour   ½ cup psyllium
½ cup pump-   husk powder
kin puree   1 tsp pumpkin
2 eggs,   pie spice
whisked   1 tsp baking
3 tbsp sugar   soda
½ cup almond   ½ tsp salt

DIRECTIONS:
In a bowl, mix the flour with sugar, husk powder, spices, salt and
baking soda and stir. Add the
rest of the ingredients, stir the
mix well, pour into 2 loaf pans
and bake at 330 degrees F for 1
h and 20 min. Cool down, slice
and serve.

NUTRITION/ LOAF:
calories 212, fat 5.4, fiber 2.3,
carbs 8.54, protein 4

BUTTER WHOLE WHEAT BUNS

Prep time: 10 min | Cooking
time: 12 min | Servings: 4 buns

INGREDIENTS:
2 tbsp whole   soda
wheat flour   2 tbsp psyllium
2 tbsp butter,   husk
melted   ¼ cup chicken
½ tsp baking   stock

DIRECTIONS:
In a bowl, mix the flour with the
melted butter and the other ingredients and knead the dough
obtain very well. Divide this into
4 balls, flatten each ball a bit, arrange on a lined baking sheet
and bake at 340 degrees F for 12
min.

NUTRITION/BUN:
calories 142, fat 4.3, fiber 3.4,
carbs 6.5, protein 2.3

MOZZARELLA RYE BAGELS

Prep time: 10 min | Cooking
time: 20 min | Servings: 4

INGREDIENTS:
1 cup rye flour   1 egg, whisked
1 cup mozza-   1 tbsp sesame
rella, shredded   seeds
1 tbsp cream   1 tbsp butter,
cheese   melted
1 tsp salt   1 tsp sugar

DIRECTIONS:
In a bowl, mix the flour with
mozzarella and the other ingredients except the sesame seeds
and butter and stir until you obtain a firm dough. Divide into
4 pieces and divide them into
donut pans. Brush them with
the butter, sprinkle with sesame
seeds and cook at 380 degrees F
for 20 min.

NUTRITION/ BAGEL:
calories 200, fat 4.3, fiber 2.3, carbs 5.4, protein 7.6

CHILI QUINOA LOAF

Prep time: 10 min | Cooking time: 25 min | Servings: 1 loaf

INGREDIENTS:

- 1 and ½ cups quinoa, cooked
- ½ cup flaxseed meal
- 2 eggs, whisked
- 1 tsp baking powder
- 1 tsp baking soda
- 1 tsp salt
- ½ cup sour cream
- 3 tbsp butter, soft
- 1 tbsp sugar
- 2 red chili peppers, minced
- ½ cup cheddar cheese, grated
- Cooking spray

DIRECTIONS:
In a bowl, mix the quinoa with flax seed meal, baking powder, baking soda and the other ingredients and stir until your obtain a dough. Knead the dough for 10 min, transfer it to a loaf pan greased with cooking spray and bake at 375 degrees F for 25 min. Cool down, slice and serve.

NUTRITION/ LOAF:
calories 200, fat 12.2, fiber 3.4, carbs 8.5, protein 5.3

SOFT RICE BREAD

Prep time: 10 min | Cooking time: 1 h and 10 min | Servings: 2 loaves

INGREDIENTS:

- 1 and ½ cups rice flour
- 1 tsp salt
- 1 tsp apple cider vinegar
- 1 tsp baking soda
- 1 tsp baking powder
- 3 tbsp psyllium husk powder
- 1 cup warm water
- 2 eggs, whisked
- 1 egg yolk, whisked
- Cooking spray

DIRECTIONS:
In a large bowl, mix the rice flour with salt, baking powder and soda and husk powder and stir. Add the eggs and the remaining ingredients except the cooking spray and stir until you obtain a dough. Knead the dough for 10 min, transfer to 2 loaf pans greased with cooking spray and bake at 350 degrees F for 1 h and 20 min. Cool the bread down, slice and serve.

NUTRITION/ LOAF:
calories 172, fat 4.4, fiber 2.3, carbs 5.5, protein 2.3

COCONUT CORN BREAD

Prep time: 10 min | Cooking time: 50 min | Servings: 1 loaf

INGREDIENTS:

- ½ cup coconut flour
- ½ cup corn flour
- 1 tsp oregano, dried
- 1 tsp basil, dried
- 5 eggs, whisked
- 6 tbsp butter, melted
- 1 tsp baking soda
- 1 tsp garlic powder
- ½ tsp black pepper
- ½ tsp salt

DIRECTIONS:
In a large bowl, mix the flour with oregano, basil and the other ingredients, stir until you obtain a dough, knead it for 10 min and transfer to a loaf pan lined with parchment paper. Bake at 340 degrees F for 50 min, cool down, slice and serve.

NUTRITION/ LOAF:
calories 172, fat 4.3, fiber 2.3, carbs 4.4, protein 6

DUTCH OVEN SPELT BREAD

Prep time: 30 min | Cooking

time: 40 min | Servings: 1 loaf

INGREDIENTS:

1 and ½ cups almond flour	1 tsp baking soda
1 and ½ cups spelt flour	½ tsp salt
1 tsp baking powder	1 tsp sugar
	1 and ½ cups warm water

DIRECTIONS:
In a bowl, mix the flour with baking powder, soda and the other ingredients, stir and knead until you obtain a dough. Cover the bowl and leave the dough to rise for 30 min. Transfer to a Dutch oven, bake at 400 degrees F for 40 min, cool down, slice and serve.

NUTRITION/ LOAF:
calories 242, fat 6.5, fiber 3.3, carbs 6.4, protein 4.3

AVOCADO WHOLE WHEAT BREAD

Prep time: 10 min | Cooking time: 40 min | Servings: 1 loaf

INGREDIENTS:

1 cup whole wheat flour	melted
1 tsp baking powder	½ tsp vanilla extract
1 tsp cinnamon powder	1 tsp lemon juice
½ cup sugar	1 cup avocado, peeled, pitted and mashed
1 egg, whisked	
4 tbsp butter,	

DIRECTIONS:
In a bowl, mix the flour with baking powder, cinnamon and the other ingredients and stir well until you obtain a dough. Knead the dough for 10 min, transfer to a loaf pan and bake it at 320 degrees F for 40 min. Cool the bread down, slice and serve.
Nutrition/ loaf: calories 254, fat 6.5, fiber 3.4, carbs 6.5, protein 6

PARMESAN RICE BREAD

Prep time: 1 h and 10 min | Cooking time: 40 min | Servings: 2 loaves

INGREDIENTS:

1 cup parmesan, grated	1 tsp baking powder
1 cup rice flour	1 tsp salt
1 and ½ cups warm water	1 tsp black pepper
1 tsp instant yeast	1 garlic clove, minced

DIRECTIONS:
In a large bowl, mix the flour with the water and the other ingredients, stir until you obtain a dough, cover the bowl and leave aside for 1 h. Divide the dough into 2 loaf pans, bake the bread at 390 degrees F for 40 min, cool down, slice and serve.

NUTRITION/ LOAF:
calories 272, fat 5.4, fiber 2.4, carbs 5.4, protein 3.4

WHOLE WHEAT CAULIFLOWER BREAD

Prep time: 10 min | Cooking time: 1 h | Servings: 1 loaf

INGREDIENTS:

5 tbsp olive oil	flower, grated
5 eggs, whisked	½ tsp salt
1 cup whole wheat flour	1 tbsp baking soda
2 cups cauli-	½ tsp black pepper

DIRECTIONS:
In a bowl, mix the cauliflower with whole wheat flour and the other ingredients, stir and knead for 10 min until you obtain an elastic dough. Transfer the dough to a loaf pan and bake at 350 degrees F for 1 h. Cool down, slice and serve.

BROCCOLI RYE BREAD

Prep time: 10 min | Cooking time: 40 min | Servings: 1 loaf

INGREDIENTS:
1 cup broccoli, grated	whisked
1 cup cheddar cheese, shredded	2 tsp baking soda
½ cup rye flour	1 tbsp warm water
5 eggs,	Cooking spray

INGREDIENTS:
In a bowl, mix the broccoli with the cheese and the other ingredients except the cooking spray, stir well and knead until you obtain a dough. Grease a loaf pan with the cooking spray, arrange the loaf inside and bake at 350 degrees F for 40 min. Cool the bread down, slice and serve.

SPINACH CORN BREAD

Prep time: 10 min | Cooking time: 40 min | Servings: 2 loaves

INGREDIENTS:
1 tbsp olive oil	water
1 tsp salt	1 tsp baking soda
½ cup spinach, chopped	1 tbsp sugar
3 cups corn flour	½ cup cheddar, shredded
1 cup warm	

DIRECTIONS:
In a bowl, mix the flour with the baking soda, sugar and the other ingredients, and stir well until you obtain an elastic dough. Transfer the dough to 2 loaf pans,

bake at 390 degrees F for 40 min, cool down, slice and serve.

NUTMEG ASPARAGUS BREAD

Prep time: 10 min | Cooking time: 45 min | Servings: 1 loaf

INGREDIENTS:
1 cup sugar	powder
1 cup avocado oil	1 tsp nutmeg, ground
2 cups corn flour	½ tsp salt
2 egg whites, whisked	Cooking spray
1 tsp baking	2 cups asparagus, steamed and chopped

DIRECTIONS:
In a large bowl, mix the flour with the sugar, oil and the other ingredients except the cooking spray, stir well until you obtain a dough, cover the bowl and leave aside for 10 min. Transfer the dough to a loaf pan greased with cooking spray and bake at 350 degrees F for 45 min. Cool the bread down, slice and serve.

EGGPLANT RYE BREAD

Prep time: 10 min | Cooking time: 1 h | Servings: 1 loaf

INGREDIENTS:
2 tbsp sugar	2 eggplants, washed and grated
½ cup warm milk	
2 eggs, whisked	1 tsp turmeric powder
1 and ½ cups rye flour	2 tsp baking powder
1 tsp salt	

Directions:
In a bowl, mix the flour with the milk and the other ingredients, stir well and transfer to a loaf pan. Bake at 350 degrees F for 1 h, cool down, slice and serve.

Nutrition/ loaf:
calories 200, fat 4.4, fiber 3.3, carbs 7.5, protein 4.3

ONION CORN BREAD

Prep time: 1 h | Cooking time: 40 min | Servings: 1 loaf

Ingredients:
6 spring onions, chopped
2 tbsp olive oil
1 yellow onion, chopped
4 cups corn flour
½ tsp salt
½ tsp white pepper
1 and ½ cups warm water
2 tsp dry yeast

Directions:
In a bowl, mix the spring onions with the oil, flour and the other ingredients, stir well, knead until you obtain a dough, cover the bowls and leave aside for 1 h. Transfer to a loaf pan, bake the bread at 375 degrees F for 40 min, cool down, slice and serve.

Nutrition/ loaf:
calories 253, fat 4.4, fiber 2.3, carbs 7.4, protein 4.3

BEAN WHOLE WHEAT BREAD

Prep time: 10 min | Cooking time: 30 min | Servings: 2 loaves

Ingredients:
2 cups corn flour
1 tsp baking soda
1 tsp salt
2 cups canned Cherokee beans, drained, rinsed and mashed
½ tsp hot paprika
2 eggs, whisked
2 tbsp olive oil
1 and ½ cups milk

Directions:
In a bowl, mix the flour with baking soda, salt, beans and the other ingredients, stir and knead until you obtain a dough. Divide this into 2 loaf pans, bake at 400 degrees F for 30 min, cool down, slice and serve.

Nutrition/ loaf:
calories 300, fat 6.5, fiber 6.9, carbs 12.2, protein 4.5

SANDWICH BREADS RECIPES

SIMPLE SANDWICH BREAD

Prep time: 2 h and 40 min | Cooking time: 40 min | Servings: 1 loaf

INGREDIENTS:

3 cups all purpose flour	4 tbsp vegetable oil
½ cup milk	2 tbsp sugar
2/3 cup hot water	1 tbsp dry yeast
	½ tsp salt

DIRECTIONS:

In a bowl, mix the flour with the yeast, water and the other ingredients, stir until you obtain a dough and transfer it to a floured working surface. Knead the dough for 10 min, transfer to a bowl, cover and leave aside to rise for 1 h. Transfer the dough to a loaf pan, cover and leave aside to rise for another 1 h and 30 min. Bake at 350 degrees F for 40 min.

NUTRITION/SLICE:

calories 120, fat 5, fiber 1, carbs 17, protein 5

GLUTEN-FREE SANDWICH BREAD

Prep time: 2 h | Cooking time: 40 min | Servings: 1 loaf

INGREDIENTS:

3 cups gluten-free almond flour	xantham gum
3 tbsp sugar	1 cup milk, warm
½ tsp salt	4 tbsp butter, soft
2 tsp instant yeast	3 eggs, whisked
1 and ¼ tsp	

DIRECTIONS:

In a bowl, mix the flour with the yeast, sugar and the other ingredients except the milk and the eggs and stir. Add the milk and eggs gradually and knead the mixture until you obtain an elastic dough. Cover the bowl and leave the dough to rise in a warm place for 1 h. Transfer to a round loaf pan, leave the dough to rise for another h and then bake at 360 degrees F for 40 min.

NUTRITION/ LOAF:

calories 150, fat 4, fiber 1, carbs 26, protein 5

TAPIOCA SANDWICH BREAD

Prep time: 10 min | Cooking time: 1 h | Servings: 1 loaf

INGREDIENTS:

2 tbsp coconut flour	2 eggs whites, whisked
½ cup tapioca flour	3 eggs, whisked
2 cups almond flour	½ tbsp apple cider vinegar
2 tsp baking powder	½ cup almond milk
1 tsp baking soda	¼ cup coconut oil, melted
1 tsp salt	

DIRECTIONS:

In a bowl, mix all the flour with baking soda, powder and the other dry ingredients and stir. In another bowl, mix the eggs with egg whites and the other wet ingredients and whisk. Combine 2 mixtures and stir until you obtain a dough. Transfer the dough to a loaf pan and bake in the preheated oven at 350 degrees F for 1 h. Cool down before serving.

NUTRITION/ LOAF:

calories 177, fat 5, fiber 2, carbs 8, protein 5

GARLIC SANDWICH BREAD

Prep time: 2 h | Cooking time: 40 min | Servings: 1 loaf

INGREDIENTS:

1 cup hot water
2 tbsp sugar
2 tsp dry yeast
¼ cup avocado oil
3 garlic cloves, minced
4 cups coconut flour
½ tsp coriander, ground
½ tsp rosemary, dried
2 tbsp butter, melted
½ tsp turmeric powder

DIRECTIONS:

In a large bowl, mix the flour with the garlic, coriander and the other ingredients except the water and the oil and stir well. Add the water and the oil gradually and knead the dough for 10 min. Leave the dough covered to rise for 1 h and 30 min in a warm place. Transfer the dough to a loaf pan, leave it to rise for 30 min more and bake at 370 degrees F for 40 min.

NUTRITION:

calories 233, fat 6, fiber 2, carbs 38, protein 5

WHOLE GRAIN SANDWICH BREAD

Prep time: 1 h and 30 min | Cooking time: 30 min | Servings: 2 loaves

INGREDIENTS:

6 cups whole wheat flour
1 tbsp dry active yeast
¼ cup honey
¼ cup olive oil
1 and ½ tbsp wheat gluten
2 tsp salt
2 and ½ cups warm water
½ tsp turmeric powder
½ tsp nutmeg, ground

DIRECTIONS:

In a bowl, mix the water with the yeast and 2 cups flour, stir and leave aside for 20 min. Add the rest of the ingredients, stir until you obtain a dough. Knead the dough for 10 min, cover the bowl and leave aside to rise for 1 h. Divide the dough into 2 loaf pans and leave them to rise for 10 more min. Bake at 360 degrees F for 30 min, cool down and serve.

Nutrition:
calories 110, fat 2.4, fiber 0.7, carbs 18.2, protein 2.3

SOURDOUGH SPELT SANDWICH BREAD

Prep time: 5 h | Cooking time: 40 min | Servings: 1 loaf

INGREDIENTS:

8 ounces sourdough starter
3 cups whole spelt flour
1 cup white flour
2 tbsp maple syrup
2 tbsp olive oil
1 cup water
1 tsp salt

DIRECTIONS:

In a bowl, mix the sourdough starter with the flour and the other ingredients, stir well and knead until you obtain a dough. Knead the dough for 10 min, cover it with plastic wrap and leave aside to rise for 4 h and 30 min. Transfer to a loaf pan, leave aside to rise for 30 min more and bake at 360 degrees F for 40 min. Cool down and serve.

NUTRITION/ LOAF:
calories 253, fat 4.4, fiber 2, carbs 25, protein 5.4

CHEESY SANDWICH BREAD

Prep time: 3 h | Cooking time: 30 min | Servings: 1 loaf

INGREDIENTS:

1 cup zucchini, shredded
1 and ½ tsp dry instant yeast
2 tbsp sugar
1 cup warm water
3 and ½ cups white flour
1 tsp salt

½ cup red onion, chopped
1 cup cheddar cheese, shredded

DIRECTIONS:

In a bowl, mix the flour with the yeast, sugar and half of the water, stir and leave aside for 30 min. Add the rest of the ingredients, stir until you obtain a dough, knead for 10 min, cover the bowl and leave aside for 2 h. Transfer to a loaf pan, leave the dough to rise for 30 min more and bake at 370 degrees F for 30 min. Cool down before serving.

NUTRITION/SLICE:

calories 223, fat 5.4, fiber 4.5, carbs 14, protein 3.4

TOMATO SANDWICH BREAD

Prep time: 2 h | Cooking time: 35 min | Servings: 2 loaves

INGREDIENTS:

6 cups white flour
1 ounce dry yeast
2 tbsp sugar
1 tsp salt
½ tsp basil, dried
½ tsp rosemary, dried
2 cups tomato juice
½ cup tomato sauce
1 tsp oregano, dried
1 tsp garlic powder
2 tbsp olive oil

DIRECTIONS:

In a bowl, mix half of the flour with the yeast, sugar, salt and tomato juice, stir and leave aside for 30 min. Add the rest of the ingredients gradually and stir until you obtain a dough. Knead the dough for 10 min, cover the bowl and leave aside for 1 h to rise. Transfer the dough to 2 loaves pan, leave the dough to rise for 30 min more and bake at 360 degrees F for 35 min. Cool the bread down, slice and serve.

NUTRITION:

calories 102, fat 1, fiber 1, carbs 20, protein 3

VEGAN SANDWICH BREAD

Prep time: 1 h and 30 min | Cooking time: 45 min | Servings: 1 loaf

INGREDIENTS:

½ cup warm water
2 tbsp agave syrup
½ cup almond milk
1 tbsp dry active yeast
3 cups organic almond flour
1 tsp salt
1 tsp sweet paprika
1 tsp turmeric powder

DIRECTIONS:

In a bowl, mix the yeast with agave syrup and water, stir and leave aside for 10 min. In another bowl, mix the flour with salt, paprika and turmeric and stir. Add yeast mix, also add the milk, stir until you obtain a dough and leave aside to rise covered for 1 h and 20 min. Transfer to a loaf pan, leave the dough to rise for 10 min more and bake at 350 degrees F for 45 min. Cool down, slice and serve.

NUTRITION:

calories 206, fat 4, fiber 1, carbs 35, protein 4

SPROUTED BREAD SANDWICH

Prep time: 10 min | Cooking time: 45 min | Servings: 2 loaves

INGREDIENTS:

6 cups sprouted wheat flour
2 tsp salt
3 tbsp honey
3 cups buttermilk
3 tbsp coconut oil, melted
1 tbsp butter, soft
1 tsp cumin, ground

DIRECTIONS:

In a bowl, mix the flour with salt, honey and the other ingredients, stir until you obtain an elastic dough, knead for 10 min and divide into 2 loaf pans. Bake at 360 degrees F for 45 min, cool down and serve.

NUTRITION:

calories 201, fat 4.5, fiber 2.3, carbs 20, protein 4

DIABETIC SANDWICH BREAD

Prep time: 10 min | Cooking time: 25 min | Servings: 1 loaf

INGREDIENTS:

1 and ½ cups almond flour	powder
3 tbsp butter, soft	½ tsp cream of tartar
1 tsp salt	6 eggs, whisked
3 tsp baking	Cooking spray

DIRECTIONS:

In a bowl, mix the flour with melted butter and the other ingredients except the cooking spray, stir well and transfer to a loaf pan greased with cooking spray. Bake at 375 degrees F for 25 min, cool down and serve.

NUTRITION:

calories 225, fat 20, fiber 2.3, carbs 0.8, protein 9.3

YOGURT SANDWICH BREAD

Prep time: 1 h | Cooking time: 40 min | Servings: 1 loaf

INGREDIENTS:

1 and ½ cups warm water	yeast
1 cup natural yogurt	1 tsp salt
1 tsp dry active	3 and ½ cups white flour

DIRECTIONS:

In a bowl, mix the yeast with 1 cup flour and 1 cup water, stir and leave aside for 10 min. Add the rest of the ingredients, stir well and knead until you obtain a dough. Leave aside the dough to rise for 1 h, transfer to a loaf pan and bake at 425 degrees F for 40 min.

NUTRITION:

calories 161, fat 1, fiber 1, carbs 33, protein 5

ARTICHOKE SANDWICH BREAD

Prep time: 20 min | Cooking time: 30 min | Servings: 1 loaf

INGREDIENTS:

10 ounces canned artichoke hearts, drained and minced	soda
	1 tsp active dry yeast
	2 and ½ cups almond flour
1 cup parmesan, grated	1 and ½ cups warm water
2 garlic cloves, minced	1 tsp basil, dried
1 tsp baking	

DIRECTIONS:

In a bowl, mix the flour with baking soda, yeast and 1.2 cup water, stir and leave aside for 15 min. Add the rest of the ingredients and stir until you obtain a dough. Knead the dough, transfer to a loaf pan and bake at 360 degrees F for 30 min.

NUTRITION:

calories 211, fat 5, fiber 2, carbs 3.4, protein 4.3

KETOGENIC SANDWICH BREAD

Prep time: 10 min | Cooking time: 25 min | Servings: 1 loaf

INGREDIENTS:

2 and ½ cups coconut flour	2 tsp baking powder
2 cups whey protein	1 and ¼ cups warm water
½ tsp instant yeast	1 tsp salt

DIRECTIONS:
In a bowl mix the flour with the protein, yeast, baking powder and salt, stir and leave aside for 10 min. Add the water, stir until you obtain a dough, transfer it to a loaf pan and bake at 400 degrees F for 25 min. Cool the bread down, slice and serve.

NUTRITION:
calories 192, fat 12, fiber 3, carbs 8, protein 18

CORNBREAD SANDWICH BREAD

Prep time: 1 h and 30 min | Cooking time: 45 min | Servings: 1 loaf

INGREDIENTS:

¼ cup honey	milk
1 cup cornmeal	3 tbsp vegetable oil
3 cups white flour	1 tsp salt
1 cup whole	2 tsp dry yeast

DIRECTIONS:
In a pan, combine the honey with milk and oil, whisk well, heat up over medium heat for 5 min and take off the heat. In a bowl, mix the flour with yeast, salt and honey mix, stir well and leave aside for 5 min. Add the rest of the ingredients, stir until you obtain a dough and then knead it for 10 min until smooth. Cover the dough with a plastic wrap and leave it in a warm place for 1 h. Transfer to a loaf pan, leave it to rise for 30 min more and then bake at 375 degrees F for 45 min.

NUTRITION:
calories 391, fat 6, fiber 4, carbs 48, protein 11

OLIVES SANDWICH BREAD

Prep time: 2 h and 30 min | Cooking time: 30 min | Servings: 1 loaf

INGREDIENTS:

3 cups all purpose flour	powder
2 tsp instant yeast	½ tsp garlic powder
1 cup warm water	½ cup kalamata olives, pitted and chopped
1 tsp salt	½ tbsp olive oil
½ tsp turmeric	

DIRECTIONS:
In a bowl, mix the flour with the yeast and the other ingredients except the water and stir well. Add the water gradually, stir and knead for 10 min until you obtain an elastic dough. Cover the dough with a plastic wrap and leave aside to rise for 1 h in a warm place. Transfer to a loaf pan and leave aside to rise for 1 more h. Bake at 375 degrees F for 30 min, cool down and serve.

NUTRITION:
calories 150, fat 3, fiber 1, carbs 26, protein 4.1

RED PEPPER SANDWICH BREAD

Prep time: 3 h | Cooking time: 25 min | Servings: 2 loaves

INGREDIENTS:

1 and ½ cups roasted red peppers, chopped	parmesan, grated
1 tsp dry yeast	1 and ½ tsp salt
2 tbsp water, warm	1 egg, whisked
1 and ½ cups	3 and ½ cups white flour
	½ cup warm milk

| 2 tsp black pepper | 2 tbsp butter, soft |

DIRECTIONS:
In a bowl, mix the yeast with 2 tbsp water, salt and ½ cups flour, stir and leave aside for 30 min. Add the rest of the ingredients except the egg and black pepper, stir and knead until you obtain an elastic dough. Cover the bowl and leave the dough aside in a warm place for 1 h. Divide the dough into 2 loaf pans and leave them to rise covered for 1 more h. Brush the loaves with the egg mixed with black pepper and bake the bread at 375 degrees F for 25 min. Cool down, slice and serve.

NUTRITION:
calories 100, fat 3, fiber 1, carbs 14, protein 4

BOULE SANDWICH BREAD

Prep time: 16 h and 10 min | Cooking time: 25 min | Servings: 1 boule bread

INGREDIENTS:
6 and ½ cups bread flour	dry yeast
2 tbsp salt	3 and ½ cups water
1 tbsp active	

DIRECTIONS:
In a bowl, mix the flour with salt and yeast. Add the water gradually and mix until you obtain an elastic dough. Transfer the dough to a floured working surface and knead it for 10 min. Shape the dough into a ball, place into a bowl and leave it aside, covered for 4 h. Transfer the dough to a floured surface again, punch it for a few min, shape into a ball again, transfer to a floured bowls, cover it and keep in the fridge for 12 h. Transfer the dough in the shape of a ball to a lined baking sheet, flatten it a bit, make some slits across the dough and bake at 400 degrees F for 30 min.

NUTRITION:
calories 200, fat 5.4, fiber 6.4, carbs 19, protein 3.4

CHARD SANDWICH BREAD

Prep time: 20 min | Cooking time: 1 h | Servings: 2 loaves

INGREDIENTS:
5 Swiss chard leaves, chopped	oil, melted ¼ cup melted butter
3 eggs, whisked	1 tsp salt 3 cups white flour
¼ cup olive oil	
1 cup cane sugar	1 tsp baking soda
½ cup stevia	1 tsp instant yeast
¼ cup coconut	

DIRECTIONS:
In a bowl, mix the yeast with flour, baking soda, salt and sugar, stir and leave aside for 10 min. Add the rest of the ingredients, stir until you obtain a dough and knead for 10 min more. Divide into 2 loaf pans lined with parchment paper and bake at 350 degrees F for 1 h. Cool down and serve.

NUTRITION:
calories 172, fat 5, fiber 3, carbs 24.4, protein 3.3

NO KNEAD SANDWICH BREAD

Prep time: 12 h and 10 min | Cooking time: 40 min | Servings: 1 loaf

INGREDIENTS:
| 3 and ½ cups white flour | 2 tsp salt |
| 1 tsp instant yeast | 1 and ½ cups warm water |

DIRECTIONS:

In a bowl mix the flour with salt and yeast. Add the water and stir until you obtain a dough. Cover the bowl and leave the dough to rise for 12 h. Transfer to a loaf pan lined with parchment paper and bake at 500 degrees F for 40 min. Cool down and serve.

NUTRITION:

calories 200, fat 5.4, fiber 2.3, carbs 12, protein 4.3

BAKING WITH A BREAD MACHINE

WHITE COUNTRY BREAD

Prep time: 10 min | Cooking time: 2 h | Servings: 1 loaf

INGREDIENTS:

2 and ½ cups white flour	powder
1 and ½ cups water	2 and ½ tsp bread machine yeast
1 cup bread flour	2 tsp sugar
1 tsp baking	1 tbsp olive oil
	1 tsp salt

DIRECTIONS:

In the bread machine, mix the flour with bread flour, water and the other ingredients, set the machine on quick setting and medium crust. Push the start button and cool the bread down before serving.

NUTRITION:

calories 122, fat 5, fiber 3.4, carbs 17, protein 2

WHOLE BREAD

Prep time: 10 min | Cooking time: 2 h | Servings: 1 loaf

INGREDIENTS:

1 and ½ cups warm water	3 tbsp coconut milk
2 tbsp avocado oil	2 tsp dry yeast
1 tsp salt	4 and ½ cups whole wheat flour
1/3 cup brown sugar	

DIRECTIONS:

In the bread machine, mix the water with the oil and the other ingredients. Cook the bread using the Whole Wheat mode and cool the bread down before serving.

NUTRITION:
calories 200, fat 4.3, fiber 5, carbs 16, protein 3.4

CEREAL BREAD

Prep time: 10 min | Cooking time: 40 min | Servings: 1 loaf

INGREDIENTS:
1 and ½ cups bread flour
1 and ½ cups warm water
2 tbsp butter
1 and ½ cups whole wheat
flour
1 cup multi-grain cereal
1 tsp salt
3 tsp sugar
2 tsp bread machine yeast

DIRECTIONS:
In your bread machine, mix the flour with the water and the other ingredients. Select Basil Cycle and medium crust and start the machine. Cool down and serve.

NUTRITION/SLICE:
calories 143, fat 4, fiber 4.4, carbs 25, protein 6

MILK BREAD

Prep time: 10 min | Cooking time: 2 h | Servings: 1 loaf

INGREDIENTS:
1 cup coconut milk
2 tbsp coconut cream
3 tbsp honey
3 tbsp butter,
soft
3 cups bread flour
1 tsp salt
2 tsp dry machine yeast

DIRECTIONS:
In the bread machine, mix the coconut milk with the cream and the other ingredients, chose the white bread setting and medium crust and start the machine. Cool down and serve.

NUTRITION:
calories 70, fat 3, fiber 2.3, carbs 7, protein 2

POTATO ROLLS

Prep time: 55 min | Cooking time: 20 min | Servings: 24 pieces

INGREDIENTS:
2 sweet potatoes, cooked, peeled and mashed
1 cup milk
3 tbsp butter,
soft
4 cups white flour
1 egg, whisked
1 tsp salt
2 tsp dry yeast

DIRECTIONS:
In the bread machine, combine the sweet potatoes with the milk and the other ingredients and use the basil dough cycle. At the end of this cycle, tear pieces of the dough, shape medium balls and arrange them in a lined baking sheet. Leave the dough to rise for 45 min and then bake at 375 degrees F for 20 min.

NUTRITION/ROLL:
calories 141, fat 6, fiber 3, carbs 17, protein 4

PRETZELS

Prep time: 20 min | Cooking time: 10 min | Servings: 12

INGREDIENTS:
1 tbsp sugar
3 cups white flour
2 tsp dry yeast
1 and ½ cups
water+ 2 quarts
1 tsp salt
1/3 cup baking soda

DIRECTIONS:
In your bread machine, mix the sugar with flour, yeast, 1 and ½ cups water and salt and set the machine to dough cycle. When the cycle is done, transfer the dough to a floured working surface, knead, divide into 12 pieces, and roll each piece into a rope. Heat up a pan with the rest of the water and the baking soda,

bring to a simmer over medium heat, add the pretzels, simmer for 2 min and transfer them to lined baking sheets. Bake at 475 degrees F for 10 min.

Nutrition/ pretzel:
calories 40, fat 2, fiber 2, carbs 6, protein 1

PIZZA DOUGH

Prep time: 10 min | Cooking time: 15 min | Servings: 2 pizzas

Ingredients:
2 tbsp olive oil
4 cups bread flour
1 and ½ cups water
1 tbsp sugar
2 tsp salt
2 tsp active yeast

Directions:
Put all the ingredients in the bread machine and select the dough cycle. When the cycle is done, take the dough and divide into 2 pizza pans. Bake the crusts at 400 degrees F for 15 min and use.

Nutrition/ pizza crust:
calories 40, fat 2, fiber 2, carbs 5, protein 1

BUTTER BREAD

Prep time: 10 min | Cooking time: 40 min | Servings: 1 loaf

Ingredients:
½ cup butter, soft
3 cups white flour
1 tsp salt
1 cup water
2 tbsp brown sugar
2 tsp active yeast

Directions:
In your bread machine, combine all the ingredients, select the Basic bread cycle and light crust and turn the machine on. When the cycle is done, cool the bread

28

down and serve.

Nutrition:
calories 152, fat 4, fiber 2, carbs 15, protein 4

MILK ONION SAVORY BREAD

Prep time: 20 min | Cooking time: 2 h | Servings: 1 loaf

Ingredients:
2 tbsp coconut oil, melted
2 tsp salt
1 and ½ cups water
1 tbsp sugar
4 cups white
flour
2 tbsp dry milk
2 tsp active yeast
4 tbsp dry onion soup mix

Directions:
Combine all the ingredients in your bread machine, select the Bread cycle and Medium crust and start the machine. Cool the bread down before serving.

Nutrition:
calories 152, fat 4, fiber 3, carbs 15, protein 7

PARMESAN BREAD

Prep time: 10 min | Cooking time: 3 h | Servings: 1 loaf

Ingredients:
2 tbsp avocado oil
3 garlic cloves, minced
1 and ½ cups water, warm
3 tbsp chives, chopped
1 tbsp basil, chopped
1 tsp salt
1 tbsp brown sugar
2 tsp active dry yeast
4 cups white flour
4 tbsp parmesan, grated

Directions:
In your bread machine, combine all the ingredients, select the basil cycle and medium crust, bake.

Nutrition: calories 102, fat 3, fiber 4, carbs 13, protein 4

JEWISH BREAD

Prep time: 2 h and 10 min | Cooking time: 1 h | Servings: 1 bread

INGREDIENTS:

1 egg yolk, whisked
1 egg white, whisked
2 tsp salt
1 cup warm water
½ cup honey
2 tbsp olive oil
4 cups white flour
2 tsp bread machine yeast

DIRECTIONS:
In your bread machine, mix the flour with yeast and the other ingredients, set the machine on Basil cycle and light crust and start the machine. When the final rise is done, set the machine on Pause, transfer the dough to a floured working surface and knead gently. Divide the dough in 3 parts, roll each part into long ropes, braid them together and tuck the ends. Transfer the bread to the bread machine and continue the cycle. Cool down and serve.

NUTRITION/ LOAF:
calories 200, fat 7, fiber 3, carbs 20, protein 7

ITALIAN BREAD

Prep time: 10 min | Cooking time: 1 h | Servings: 1 loaf

INGREDIENTS:

4 garlic cloves, minced
3 tbsp soft butter
1 bulb roasted garlic
1 cup milk
½ cup cheddar, grated
3 cups white bread flour
1 tsp salt
2 tbsp sugar
1 tsp garlic powder
1 tsp dry active yeast

DIRECTIONS:
Squeeze roasted garlic, mash the flesh and put it in a bowl. In your bread machine mix all the other ingredients, set the machine on Basic White cycle and Medium Crust and start the program. When the last kneading cycle starts, add the roasted garlic as well. Make the bread and cool down before serving.

NUTRITION:
calories 140, fat 4, fiber 3, carbs 16, protein 4

VEGGIE BREAD

Prep time: 10 min | Cooking time: 2 h | Servings: 1 loaf

INGREDIENTS:

¼ cup spring onions, chopped
½ cup water
¼ cup green bell pepper, chopped
2 tbsp chives, chopped
2 cups white flour
1 tbsp butter
1 tsp Creole seasoning
1 tbsp sugar
1 tsp salt
1 tsp active dry yeast

DIRECTIONS:
In the bread machine, mix all the ingredients, select the white bread cycle and medium crust and start the machine. Cool the bread down and serve.

NUTRITION:
calories 47, fat 3, fiber 3, carbs 7, protein 1

OATMEAL BREAD

Prep time: 10 min | Cooking time: 2 h and 30 min | Servings: 1 loaf

INGREDIENTS:

2 tsp salt	1 tbsp molasses
2 tbsp butter, soft	½ cup old-fashioned oats
1 cup warm water	1 egg, whisked
3 tbsp honey	2 tsp dry yeast

DIRECTIONS:
In your bread machine, mix all the ingredients. Set the machine on White bread cycle and Medium crust and push the start button. When the bread is done, cool down and serve.

NUTRITION:
calories 162, fat 7, fiber 4, carbs 17, protein 5

ROMANO CHEESE BREAD

Prep time: 10 min | Cooking time: 2 h | Servings: 1 loaf

INGREDIENTS:

1 cup water	2 tbsp sugar
½ cup Romano cheese, shredded	1 tsp salt
3 cups white flour	1 tsp black pepper
1 tbsp oregano, chopped	2 tsp active yeast
	2 tbsp olive oil

DIRECTIONS:
In your bread machine, mix the flour and the other ingredients, select the White bread cycle and light crust and push the start button. Cool the bread down, slice and serve.

NUTRITION/SLICE:
calories 70, fat 3, fiber 3, carbs 7, protein 2

CHEDDAR, OLIVES AND TOMATO BREAD

Prep time: 10 min | Cooking time: 1 h | Servings: 1 loaf

INGREDIENTS:

½ cup cheddar cheese, grated	butter
3 tbsp black olives, pitted and sliced	1 cup milk
½ cup sun-dried tomatoes, chopped	3 cups white bread flour
3 tbsp soft	1 tsp salt
	2 tbsp sugar
	1 tsp dry active yeast

DIRECTIONS:
In your bread machine, mix the cheese with the olives and the other ingredients, set the machine on Basic White cycle and Medium Crust and start the program. Make the bread and cool down before serving.

NUTRITION:
calories 130, fat 3.2, fiber 3, carbs 11.6, protein 4

PARMESAN AND CUCUMBER BREAD

Prep time: 10 min | Cooking time: 2 h | Servings: 1 loaf

INGREDIENTS:

2 tbsp olive oil	water, warm
½ cup parmesan, grated	1 tsp salt
1 cup cucumber, minced	2 tsp active dry yeast
1 and ½ cups	4 cups white flour

DIRECTIONS:
In your bread machine, combine all the ingredients, select the basil cycle and medium crust, bake, cool down and serve.

NUTRITION:
calories 132, fat 4.5, fiber 3.2, carbs 13, protein 4

SPRING ONIONS AND ZUCCHINI BREAD

Prep time: 10 min | Cooking time: 2 h | Servings: 1 loaf

INGREDIENTS:

¼ cup spring onions, chopped
½ cup water
¼ cup spring onions, chopped
3 cups bread flour
1 tbsp olive oil
1 tsp salt
1 tsp active dry yeast

DIRECTIONS:

In the bread machine, mix all the ingredients, select the white bread cycle and medium crust and start the machine. Cool the bread down and serve.

NUTRITION:

calories 87, fat 6.5, fiber 3, carbs 7, protein 3.4

MILK AND BASIL BREAD

Prep time: 10 min | Cooking time: 2 h | Servings: 1 loaf

INGREDIENTS:

1 cup almond milk
1 tbsp sugar
1 tbsp basil, chopped
3 tbsp butter, soft
3 cups bread flour
1 tsp salt
2 tsp dry machine yeast

DIRECTIONS:

In the bread machine, mix the milk with the sugar and the other ingredients, chose the white bread setting and medium crust and start the machine. Cool down and serve.

NUTRITION:

calories 100, fat 3, fiber 4, carbs 7, protein 3

MINT BREAD

Prep time: 10 min | Cooking time: 2 h | Servings: 1 loaf

INGREDIENTS:

1 cup warm water
1 tbsp mint, chopped
3 tbsp honey
3 tbsp coconut oil, melted
3 and ½ cups white flour
1 tsp salt
2 tsp dry machine yeast

DIRECTIONS:

In the bread machine, mix the warm water with mint and the other ingredients, select the white bread setting and medium crust and start the machine. Cool down and serve.

NUTRITION:

calories 70, fat 3, fiber 2.3, carbs 7, protein 2

SWEET BAKE

ALMOND BLACKBERRIES BREAD

Prep time: 10 min | Cooking time: 1 h | Servings: 1 loaf

INGREDIENTS:

2 cups almond flour	2 eggs, whisked
2 tbsp almonds, chopped	1 and ½ cups almond flour
½ cup brown sugar	¼ cup butter, melted
2 tsp baking powder	1 tbsp vanilla extract
1 tsp active yeast	1 cup blackberries, mashed
	Cooking spray

DIRECTIONS:

In a bowl, mix the flour with the baking powder, yeast and the other ingredients, stir until you obtain a smooth dough, pour it into a loaf pan greased with cooking spray. Bake at 400 degrees F for 1 h, cool down, slice and serve.

NUTRITION/SLICE:

calories 276, fat 7, fiber 3, carbs 5, protein 7

VANILLA RASPBERRIES BREAD

Prep time: 10 min | Cooking time: 1 h | Servings: 1 loaf

INGREDIENTS:

2 cups white flour	milk
1 tsp baking powder	¼ cup ghee, melted
¾ cup erythritol	2 cups raspberries
½ tsp salt	2 tsp vanilla extract
1 egg	¼ cup vegetable oil
¾ cup almond	

DIRECTIONS:

In a bowl, mix the flour with the baking powder, salt and all the other ingredients and stir. Pour this into a lined loaf pan and bake at 350 degrees F for 1 h. Cool the bread down, slice and serve.

NUTRITION:

calories 253, fat 5.7, fiber 3, carbs 5, protein 7

STRAWBERRY BREAD

Prep time: 10 min | Cooking time: 50 min | Servings: 2 loaves

INGREDIENTS:

4 cups almond flour	1 tbsp nutmeg, ground
2 cups strawberries, chopped	4 eggs, whisked
1 tsp baking powder	1 cup coconut oil, melted
1 cup sugar	Cooking spray

DIRECTIONS:

In a bowl, mix the flour with baking powder, berries and the other ingredients except the cooking spray. Pour this into 2 loaf pans greased with cooking spray, bake at 350 degrees F for 50 min, cool the breads down, slice and serve.

NUTRITION:

calories 221, fat 7.3, fiber 4.4, carbs 5, protein 3

PLUM AND COCONUT BREAD

Prep time: 10 min | Cooking time: 50 min | Servings: 2 loaves

INGREDIENTS:

1 cup plums, pitted and chopped	flour
½ cup coconut, shredded	¼ tsp baking powder
1 cup coconut	½ cup butter, soft
	½ tsp salt

| 1 and ¼ cups sugar | 1/3 cup coconut milk |
| ½ tsp vanilla extract | 2 eggs, whisked |

DIRECTIONS:
In a bowl, mix the flour with baking powder, coconut flour, coconut and the other ingredients and stir well. Pour into 2 lined loaf pans and bake at 350 degrees F for 50 min. Cool the breads down, slice and serve them.

NUTRITION/SLICE:
calories 219, fat 8.4, fiber 3.5, carbs 6, protein 4

LEMON BREAD

Prep time: 10 min | Cooking time: 50 min | Servings: 2 loaves

INGREDIENTS:
2/3 cup butter, melted	milk
1 and ½ cups brown sugar	2 tbsp lemon zest, grated
4 eggs, whisked	2 tbsp lemon juice
3 tsp baking soda	3 cups almond flour
1 cup coconut	Cooking spray

DIRECTIONS:
In a bowl, mix the flour with sugar, baking soda and the other dry ingredients and stir. Add the wet ingredients as well, and stir really well. Pour into 2 loaf pans greased with cooking spray and bake at 350 degrees F for 50 min. Cool the breads down, slice and serve.

NUTRITION:
calories 203, fat 7.4, fiber 3.4, carbs 8.7, protein 6

LEMON RHUBARB BREAD

Prep time: 10 min | Cooking time: 40 min | Servings: 2 loaves

INGREDIENTS:
1 cup almond milk	flour
1 tsp vanilla extract	2 cups rhubarb, chopped
1 tbsp lemon juice	½ tsp salt
2/3 cup vegetable oil	1 tsp baking powder
2 eggs, whisked	½ tsp cinnamon powder
1 cup sugar	1 tbsp butter, melted
3 cups almond	Cooking spray

DIRECTIONS:
In a bowl, mix the milk with vanilla, lemon juice and the other ingredients except the cooking spray and stir well. Pour into 2 loaf pans greased with cooking spray. Bake at 350 degrees F for 40 min, cool down, slice and serve.

NUTRITION/SLICE:
calories 203, fat 4.7, fiber 2, carbs 4, protein 3.4

GINGER CANTALOUPE BREAD

Prep time: 10 min | Cooking time: 1 h | Servings: 2 loaves

INGREDIENTS:
4 tbsp sugar	1 tbsp nutmeg, ground
3 eggs, whisked	½ tsp almond extract
1 cup avocado oil	1 and ½ tsp baking powder
1 tbsp ginger, minced	½ cup ghee, melted
1 and ½ cups cantaloupe puree	3 cups almond flour

DIRECTIONS:
In a bowl, mix the flour with ginger, nutmeg and all the other ingredients and stir really well. Pour into 2 lined loaf pans and bake at 360 degrees F for 1 h. Cool the breads down, slice.

calories 211, fat 5.8, fiber 4.3, carbs 6, protein 3.8

HONEY BREAD

Prep time: 10 min | Cooking time: 50 min | Servings: 1 loaf

INGREDIENTS:

1 tbsp baking soda	1 cup water
2 tbsp stevia	1 tsp nutmeg, ground
2 tbsp honey	4 tbsp coconut oil, melted
3 cups all purpose flour	1 tsp salt
1 cup beer	

DIRECTIONS:
In a bowl, mix the flour with nutmeg, baking soda and the other ingredients and stir well. Transfer this to a lined loaf pan and bake at 350 degrees F for 50 min.

NUTRITION:
calories 102, fat 3.4, fiber 4.5, carbs 7.4, protein 3.4

GINGER AND NUTMEG BREAD

Prep time: 10 min | Cooking time: 40 min | Servings: 1 loaf

INGREDIENTS:

1 tsp sugar	flour
1/3 cup warm water	¼ cup molasses
1 tsp active dry yeast	2 tsp salt
2 tbsp coconut oil, melted	2 tbsp ground ginger
1 cup milk	2 tbsp butter, melted
3 and ¼ cups all purpose	1 cup brown sugar

DIRECTIONS:
In a bowl, mix the sugar with the water, yeast and the other ingredients, stir until you obtain a dough and transfer to a working surface. Knead the dough for 10 min, cover it and leave aside to rise for 1 h. Transfer the dough to a loaf pan, cover the pan and leave to rise for 1 more h. Introduce the pan in the oven at 350 degrees F and bake for 40 min. Cool down, slice and serve.

NUTRITION:
calories 200, fat 1.4, fiber 2.3, carbs 5.4, protein 5.5

CHOCOLATE BREAD

Prep time: 15 min | Cooking time: 1 h | Servings: 2 loaves

INGREDIENTS:

2 oz dark chocolate, chopped	½ cup butter
2 tbsp sugar	2 eggs, whisked
1 tsp almond extract	Zest of 1 orange, grated
3 cups almond flour	4 tbsp orange juice
1 tsp baking powder	4 tbsp almond milk
1 tsp salt	

DIRECTIONS:
Heat up a small pan over medium heat, add the chocolate, sugar and almond extract and heat up for 2 min. In a bowl, mix the flour with baking powder, chocolate and the other ingredients and stir well. Pour this into 2 small loaf pans and bake at 300 degrees F for 1 h. Cool the breads down, slice and serve.

NUTRITION/ SLICE:
calories 172, fat 4.3, fiber 3.4, carbs 7.6, protein 3.4

BANANA BREAD

Prep time: 15 min | Cooking time: 1 h and 10 min | Servings: 2 loaves

INGREDIENTS:

2 bananas,	peeled and

chopped
2 cups white flour
½ cup melted butter
½ cup coconut oil, melted
½ cup almonds, chopped
½ tsp baking powder
½ tsp almond extract
1 cup sugar
2 eggs
1 tsp baking soda

DIRECTIONS:
In a bowl, mix the bananas with the flour, melted butter and the other ingredients and stir really well. Divide the mix into 2 lined pans and bake in the preheated oven at 325 degrees F for 1 h and 10 min. Cool the breads down, slice and serve.

NUTRITION:
calories 211, fat 4.3, fiber 3.2, carbs 6, protein 5.4

CHERRY BREAD

Prep time: 15 min | Cooking time: 1 h | Servings: 1 loaf

INGREDIENTS:
2 cups cherries, pitted and chopped
2 cups white flour
1 cup sugar
2 eggs, whisked
2 tsp baking soda
½ tsp salt
½ cup coconut oil, melted
¼ cup cherry juice
1 tsp almond extract
1 tsp vanilla extract

DIRECTIONS:
In a bowl, mix the cherries with flour, sugar and the other ingredients and stir well. Grease and flour a loaf pan and pour the batter in it. Introduce in the oven at 350 degrees F and bake for 1 h. Cool the bread down, slice.

NUTRITION:
calories 162, fat 4.5, fiber 4.3, carbs 12, protein 4.3

VANILLA BREAD

Prep time: 15 min | Cooking time: 1 h | Servings: 1 loaf

INGREDIENTS:
1 cup sugar
2 eggs, whisked
1/3 cup melted butter
2 tsp vanilla extract
1 tsp baking soda
1 tsp nutmeg, ground
1 tsp cinnamon powder, ground
1 tsp salt
½ cup coconut milk
½ cup white flour
2 tbsp grated lemon zest

DIRECTIONS:
In a bowl, mix the sugar with eggs and the other ingredients and whisk really well. Pour this into a loaf pan and bake at 360 degrees F for 1 h. Cool the bread down, slice and serve.

NUTRITION/SLICE:
calories 162, fat 4.3, fiber 2.3, carbs 4.5, protein 2.3

BLACKBERRY AVOCADO BREAD

Prep time: 10 min | Cooking time: 50 min | Servings: 1 loaf

INGREDIENTS:
2 cups white flour
2 avocados, peeled, pitted and mashed
1 cup blackberries
1/3 cup honey
1 tsp baking
soda
1 tsp baking powder
1 tsp salt
1 tsp nutmeg, ground
1 tsp vanilla extract
2 eggs

DIRECTIONS:
In a bowl mix the flour with the honey, baking soda and the other ingredients and whisk well. Pour into a loaf pan and bake at 350 degrees F for 50 min. Cool

the bread down, slice and serve.

NUTRITION:
calories 162, fat 4.3, fiber 3, carbs 5.1, protein 2.3

APPLE BREAD

Prep time: 15 min | Cooking time: 1 h | Servings: 1 loaf

INGREDIENTS:
1 cup brown sugar
2 cups white flour
2 tsp baking soda
4 tbsp milk
½ cup butter, softened
1 tsp almond extract
1 cup apples, cored and chopped
1 tsp cinnamon powder
2 eggs
1 tsp salt

DIRECTIONS:
In a large bowl, mix the flour with the sugar, baking soda and the other ingredients and stir well. Pour this into a lined loaf pan and bake at 350 degrees F for 1 h. Cool the bread down, slice and serve.

NUTRITION:
calories 121, fat 3.2, fiber 2.3, carbs 5.4, protein 2

SWEET RED VELVET BREAD

Prep time: 20 min | Cooking time: 50 min | Servings: 1 loaf

INGREDIENTS:
3 eggs
1/3 cup vegetable oil
½ cup pumpkin flesh
1 red velvet cake mix
1 tbsp sugar
½ cup milk

DIRECTIONS:
In a bowl, mix the eggs with cake mix and the other ingredients and whisk well. Pour the batter into a loaf pan, introduce in the oven at 350 degrees F and bake

for 50 min. Cool the bread down, slice and serve.

NUTRITION:
calories 152, fat 4.3, fiber 2.3, carbs 11, protein 3.2

GREEN TEA BREAD

Prep time: 1 h and 10 min | Cooking time: 1 h | Servings: 1 loaf

INGREDIENTS:
2 and ½ tbsp sugar
3 cups white flour
1 cup almond milk
2 eggs, whisked
1 tbsp green tea powder
¾ tbsp salt
2 tbsp butter softened
1 tsp cocoa powder
1 tsp vanilla extract
1 tsp instant yeast

DIRECTIONS:
In a bowl, mix the sugar with flour and the other ingredients except the milk and stir. Add the milk gradually, stir and knead until you obtain a dough. Cover the dough and leave it aside to rise for 1 h. Transfer to a loaf pan and bake at 375 degrees F for 30 min. Cool the bread down, slice and serve.

NUTRITION:
calories 187, fat 3.4, fiber 2.3, carbs 12, protein 5.4

PEAR AND BLUEBERRIES BREAD

Prep time: 15 min | Cooking time: 1 h | Servings: 1 loaf

INGREDIENTS:
1 cup pears, cored and chopped
½ cup blueberries
¾ cup sugar
4 eggs, whisked
2/3 cups vegetable oil

1/3 cup melted butter
1 tbsp lemon juice
1 tsp baking powder
1 tbsp grated lemon zest
2 and ½ cups white flour
½ tsp salt

DIRECTIONS:
In a large bowl, mix the pears with berries, sugar and the other ingredients and stir really well. Pour this into a lined loaf pan and bake at 350 degrees F for 1 h. Cool down, slice and serve.

NUTRITION:
calories 182, fat 2.3, fiber 3.3, carbs 7, protein 2.3

APRICOT BREAD

Prep time: 2 h | Cooking time: 1 h | Servings: 1 loaf

INGREDIENTS:
2 tbsp sugar
2 cups white flour
1 tsp dry yeast
1 egg
½ cup warm coconut milk
1 tsp vanilla extract
2 tbsp coconut oil, melted
A pinch of salt
½ cup orange juice
1 cup apricots, chopped
1 cup cream cheese softened

DIRECTIONS:
In a bowl, mix the flour with yeast and the other ingredients except the cream cheese and milk and stir. Add the rest of the ingredients, stir and knead until you obtain a soft dough. Leave the dough to rise for 1 h, transfer to a lined loaf pan, leave aside to rise for another h and bake at 375 degrees F for 1 h. Cool the bread down, slice and serve.

NUTRITION:
calories 200, fat 6.5, fiber 3, carbs 7, protein 2

MEXICAN BREAD

Prep time: 1 h and 15 min | Cooking time: 1 h | Servings: 1 loaf

INGREDIENTS:
2 tsp dry yeast
4 cups white flour
2/3 cup sugar
1 cup coconut milk
½ cup butter
1 tsp vanilla extract
1 tsp salt
2 eggs, whisked
1 tsp almond extract

DIRECTIONS:
In a bowl, mix the flour with the yeast and the other ingredients except the coconut milk and stir. Add the milk, stir until you obtain a dough, cover and leave aside for 1 h. Transfer the dough to a lined loaf pan and bake at 375 degrees F for 1 h. Cool the bread down, slice and serve.

NUTRITION:
calories 162, fat 2.3, fiber 3.4, carbs 7.5, protein 2.3

CONCLUSION

Baking bread can be a fun and interesting activity you can do in the comfort of your own home and with all your family. You can mix and use so many amazing ingredients and you can obtain so many tasty breads. This recipes collection will totally change the way to see bread making and it will become your new best friend in the kitchen when it comes to this activity.

The recipes you discovered here are so well written and in such a clear manner that can actually impress you. The ingredients used in all these recipes are simple ones, easy to find at any grocery store and accessible of each and every one of us.

All these bread recipes are rich, textured and so delightful that you will end up making them all and recommending this great journal to others as well. Trust us! It has already gained so many fans all over the world.

So what are you waiting for? Get your copy today and start baking with love and passion the best breads of your life. Enjoy them all and share them with your friends and family right away!

RECIPE INDEX

Lemon Bread, 33
Ginger and Nutmeg Bread, 34
Apple Bread, 36

BUTTERMILK
Irish Loaf, 10
Sprouted Bread Sandwich, 22

BUTTER
Mexican Rustic Loaf, 8
American Loaf, 9
Spiced Rustic Bread, 9
Russian Bread, 11
Herbed Loaf, 12
Coconut Corn Bread, 16
Easy Gluten-free Sandwich Bread, 20
Butter Bread, 28
Banana Bread, 34
Pear and Blueberries Bread, 36

CANE SUGAR
Chard Sandwich Bread, 25

CANTALOUPE
Ginger Cantaloupe Bread, 33

CARAWAY SEEDS
Rustic German Bread, 10

CAULIFLOWER
Whole Wheat Cauliflower Bread, 17

CEREAL
Cereal Bread, 27

CHARD
Chard Sandwich Bread, 25

CHEDDAR
Rustic Cheese Bread, 13
Broccoli Rye Bread, 18
Kale Corn Bread, 18
Cheesy Sandwich Bread, 21
Italian Bread, 29
Cheddar, Olives and Tomato Bread, 30

CHERRIES
Cherry Bread, 35

CHIVES
Herbed Loaf, 12

CHOCOLATE
Chocolate Bread, 34

COCONUT FLOUR
Flax Bread, 14
Coconut Corn Bread, 16
Garlic Sandwich Bread, 20
Ketogenic Sandwich Bread, 23
Plum and Coconut Bread, 32

COCONUT MILK
Milk Bread, 27
Plum and Coconut Bread, 32
Lemon Bread, 33
Vanilla Bread, 35
Apricot Bread, 37
Mexican Bread, 37

COCONUT OIL
Strawberry Bread, 32

COFFEE
Russian Bread, 11

CORIANDER
Spiced Rustic Bread, 9

CORN FLOUR
Corn Shortbread, 14
Coconut Corn Bread, 16
Kale Corn Bread, 18
Nutmeg Asparagus Bread, 18
Onion Corn Bread, 19
Bean Whole Wheat Bread, 19

CORNMEAL
Cornbread Sandwich Bread, 24

CORN SYRUP
Russian Bread, 11

CORN STARCH
Simple Baguette, 12

CREAM CHEESE
Apricot Bread, 37

CUCUMBER
Parmesan and Cucumber Bread, 30

CUMIN
French Loaf, 11
Crispy Hungarian Bread, 12

EGGPLANT
Eggplant Rye Bread, 18

FENNEL SEEDS
Russian Bread, 11

FLAXSEED MEAL
Flax Bread, 14
Flax Stevia Bread, 14
Chili Quinoa Loaf, 16

GARLIC
Garlic Sandwich Bread, 20
Italian Bread, 29

GHEE
Corn Shortbread, 14
Coconut Raspberries Bread, 32

GINGER
Spiced Rustic Bread, 9
Ginger and Nutmeg Bread, 34

GREEN TEA
Green Tea Bread, 36

HONEY
Rustic Honey Bread, 8
American Loaf, 9
Spiced Rustic Bread, 9
Rustic German Bread, 10
Herbed Loaf, 12
Whole Grain Sandwich Bread, 21
Sprouted Bread Sandwich, 22
Cornbread Sandwich Bread, 24
Jewish Bread, 29
Oatmeal Bread, 29
Mint Bread, 31

LEMON
Lemon Bread, 33
Lemon Rhubarb Bread, 33

LIME
Ethiopian Bread, 9

MARGARINE
Irish Loaf, 10

MILK
Crusty Bread, 8
Mexican Rustic Loaf, 8
American Loaf, 9
Indian Breads, 10
Herbed Loaf, 12
Eggplant Rye Bread, 18
Bean Whole Wheat Bread, 19
Simple Sandwich Bread, 20
Cornbread Sandwich Bread, 24
Red Pepper Sandwich Bread, 24
Potato Rolls, 27
Milk Onion Savory Bread, 28
Italian Bread, 29
Cheddar, Olives and Tomato Bread, 30
Ginger and Nutmeg Bread, 34
Sweet Red Velvet Bread, 36

MINT
Mint Bread, 31

MOZZARELLA
Mozzarella Rye Bagels, 15

NUTMEG
French Loaf, 11
Ginger and Nutmeg Bread, 34

OATS
Oatmeal Bread, 29

OLIVE OIL
Pita Bread, 10

OLIVES
Olives Sandwich Bread, 24
Cheddar, Olives and Tomato Bread, 30